Down from His Glory

THE LOVE STORY OF CHRISTMAS

A MUSICAL CREATED AND
ARRANGED BY **MIKE SPECK**

ORCHESTRATED BY LARI GOSS

Dec 9 5pm

*Practice Tuesday
night before
thanksgiving*

CONTENTS

Down from His Glory

includes
Carol of the Bells
O Come, O Come, Emmanuel
O Come, Let Us Adore Him

Arr. by Mike Speck

With energy! ♩. = ca. 64
*"Carol of the Bells"

*"O Come, O Come, Emmanuel"

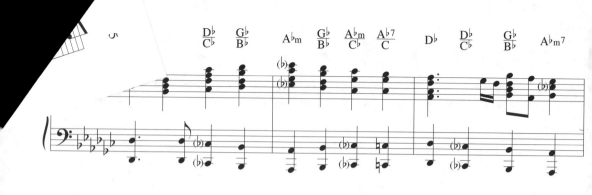

83

in - to this world He came for you and

Fm | E♭/G | A♭6 | E♭/B♭ | B°7 Cm | Fm | B♭13

86

me. The Lord de - scend - ed, God's

f

E♭ | E♭/D♭ | C♭ | A♭m

90

love_____ ex - tend - ed to ev - 'ry

F⌀7 | E♭/B♭ | Fm/B♭ E♭/B♭

Light of the Stable

Words and Music by
STEVE RHYMER
and ELIZABETH RHYMER
Arr. by Mike Speck

(Music begins)

WORSHIP LEADER: Down from His glory, came the King—the One who would save His people from their sins. This is the season we celebrate His birth and what that means to all of us. Let the celebration begin! Let rejoicing break out! All hail King Jesus!

14

16

18

CD: 9

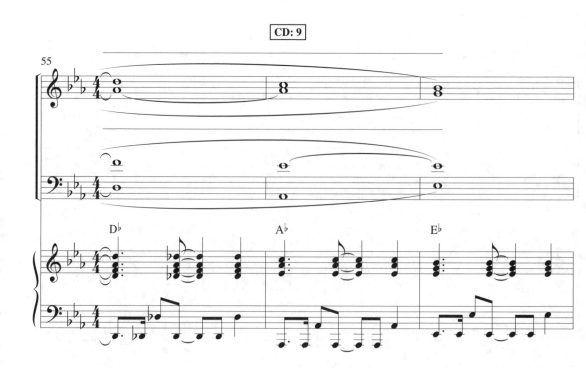

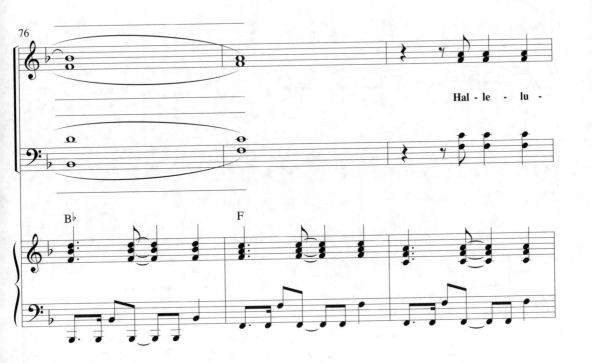

Hal La La La (Joy to the World)

with

Alleluia, Alleluia (Peace to All Men)

Arr. by Mike Speck

WORSHIP LEADER *(without music)*: "Hallelujah!" *(music begins)* simply means "Praise God!" We praise Him for the light ever-shining from the stable in Bethlehem—the light that pierces brilliantly across every corner of the earth. And how do we know? Because Christmas is celebrated all around the world; people from every nation, every city and every village, will be joyously singing the songs of Christmas. Every music style, every possible instrument will herald the news that Jesus Christ is born, from the bagpipes of Scotland to the djembe *(prounounced JEM-bay)* of West Africa, from the sitar of Calcutta, to the steal drums of Jamaica!

24

CD: 12 *". . . steal drums of Jamaica!"*

"Hal La La La (Joy to the World)"
CHILDREN'S CHOIR *unis.*

Hal - la - la - la sing-ing joy to the world! Hal - la - la - la sing-ing joy to the world!

Hal - la - la - la sing-ing joy to the world the Lord is come.

Hal - la - la - la sing-ing joy to the world! Hal - la - la - la sing-ing joy to the world!

31

bring to you___ good news of joy   a

C   Dm/C   C   Dm/C   C

33

Sav - ior comes___ as a ba - by boy,   the   lit - tle ba - by is Christ, the

C   G7   C   G7

35 CD: 14

Lord.___

F   G/F

Five Little Fingers

Words and Music by
STEPHEN THOMAS HILL and
MONICA LaVONNE STILES
*Arr. by Mike Speck
and Cliff Duren*

WORSHIP LEADER: He came from the glorious kingdom. *(Music begins)* From His perfect, eternal throne, in a very plain, ordinary way, the Lord of Glory entered our world. Once adorned in royal robes, now wrapped in swaddling clothes. Once omnipotent, now defenseless and totally dependent upon His teenage mother. The hands that once formed the heavens, carved the mountains and forged the seas . . . are now so tiny, so innocent . . . weak and fragile. Gently they reach up out of a lowly manger.

"...a lowly manger."

CHILDREN'S CHOIR *unis.*

One two three four five lit-tle fin-gers on His hand;

Son of God, Mar-y's lit-tle Man. Born in a man-ger,

gen-tle as a lamb. My heart's in the five lit-tle fin-gers of His

32

CHILDREN'S SOLO
(Opt. CHILDREN'S CHOIR)

hand.   There was   no   room   with-

in   the inn__   when   they   came   to   Beth - le - hem.__

And   in a sta - ble,   Ba - by came.__   Lit - tle   Je - sus

CD: 17

CHILDREN'S CHOIR unis.

was__   His__   name.   One two three four

It's the Messiah

Words and Music by
DON POTTER
Arr. by Mike Speck

...DER *(without music)*: The little fingers and hands *(music begins)* of ...ild were the hands of God reaching out to each of our hearts. Beyond our ability to comprehend, the Creator is now a part of creation. He who is larger than all the galaxies and beyond, now housed in and limited to a human body. *(Pause)* He emptied Himself of His glory, and journeyed from eternity to Bethlehem. There is no way for us to imagine what that must have been like.

36

38

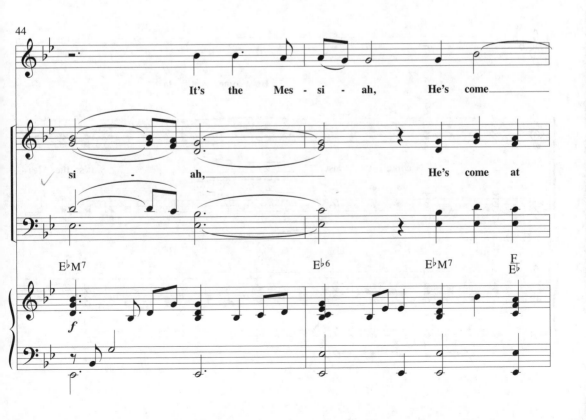

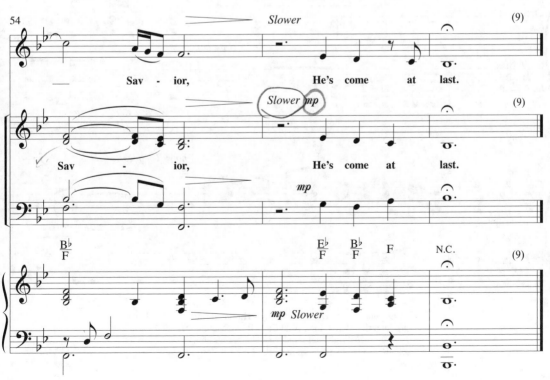

Heaven Rejoices

with
O Come, All Ye Faithful

Words and Music by
STEPHEN THOMAS HILL
and DARYL KENNETH WILLIAMS
Arr. by Mike Speck

WORSHIP LEADER *(without music)*: Messiah has come *(music begins)* . . .
Jesus, our Savior . . . The Son of the Highest . . . fully God, yet fully man . . .
the Word became flesh and dwelt among us. The invisible One became the
revealed One because He was the Promised One . . . and He is the saving
One. He comes from Heaven with salvation for all who will believe.

46

48

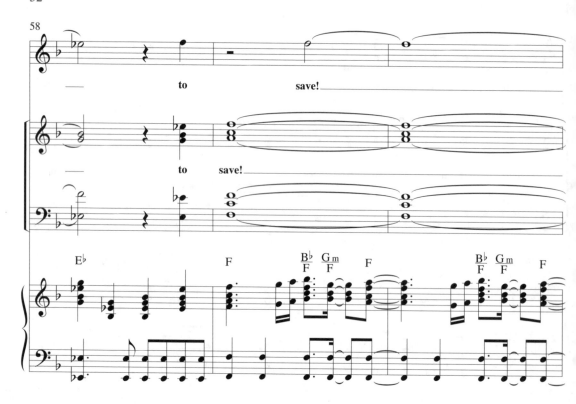

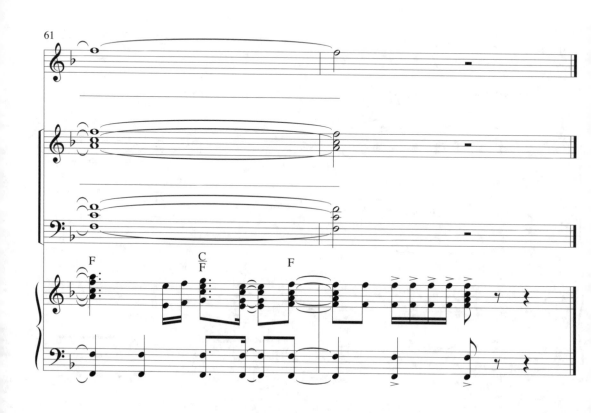

Carols of Christmas

includes

Joy to the World
Hark! the Herald Angels Sing
O Come, All Ye Faithful
O Holy Night!
Silent Night! Holy Night!

Arr. by Mike Speck

WORSHIP LEADER *(music begins)*: Let's all join the rejoicing. Sing along with us! *(Invite the congregation to stand and sing the first three carols. Seat them for "O Holy Night!" and "Silent Night! Holy Night!")*

*"Hark! the Herald Angels Sing"

Hark! the her - ald an - gels sing,___ "Glo - ry to the
new - born King! Peace on earth and mer - cy mild,___
God and sin - ners rec - on - ciled." Joy - ful, all ye

56

23

CD: 27

*"O Come, All Ye Faithful"

come___ ye to Beth - le - hem.

Come and be - hold Him born the King of

an - gels. O, come let us a - dore Him. O,

60

Pat-a-Pan Underscore
Pat-a-Pan

includes

O Little Town of Bethlehem
For unto Us a Child Is Born
Sing We Now of Christmas

Arr. by Mike Speck

WORSHIP LEADER *(without music)*: The wonderful carols of Christmas . . . they are so endearing. These familiar melodies from distant worlds somehow connect us together and cause our minds to flood with all kinds of memories and feelings. When we live in a world of ever changing trends and passing fads, *(music begins)* why would the first few notes of a little ancient carol from Germany or England or France warm our hearts and cause us to smile inside as the melody lingers? Many of us have never given any thought to how old our most beloved Christmas carols really are. Songs have been sung about the wondrous birth of Jesus for hundreds of years. Can you think of any other person in all of history who has been immortalized, esteemed and revered through so much music? We have found songs regarding the birth of Christ that date back to the 4th century. I invite you to step back in time to a small country church in France. The year is 1760, and as you sit with your family on a wintery Christmas Eve, you just might hear something like this . . .

PLEASE NOTE: Copying of this product is NOT covered by CCLI licenses. For CCLI information call 1-800-234-2446.

68

70

lis - ten as you play for a joy - ful Christ - mas day.

lis - ten as you play Christ - mas day.

CD: 34

3. God and

3. God and

He Loved Us More Underscore
He Loved Us More

with
More than Wonderful

Words and Music by
GERON DAVIS
Arr. by Mike Speck

(Without music)

WORSHIP LEADER: Well, it's Christmas. The best-known and best-loved time of the year. When family and friends get together to reminisce of days gone by . . . to laugh . . . to love . . . to eat . . . to give gifts to one another and maybe attend a Christmas performance or a candlelight service. *(Music begins)* Those of us who have grown up in church, have watched the reenactments of the Christmas story change quite a bit over the years. We've gone from homemade costumes and props to wonderfully built sets and historically accurate clothing. Do you remember when you were a kid and you raided your dad's closet for a striped bathrobe so you could play a shepherd . . . and you put a six-foot robe on your four-foot body? Remember wearing a paper crown covered in glitter to play one of the Wise Men? Or how even the most active giggly little girls seemed to have a calmness about them as they poked their heads through the cut-out holes of their mother's white sheets and stuck a coat hanger down their backs trimmed in silver or gold tinsel for their lopsided halos . . . and borrowing someone's baby doll to represent Jesus? But everyone, young and old in the room seemed to know who that makeshift manger really held and what truly mattered—that two thousand years ago heaven came to earth . . . Deity put on the robe of humanity. May the story of the birth of Jesus never become so familiar that it no longer moves us or amazes us. On a night emblazoned by a magnificent star, a child was born like no child ever before . . . or since . . . or ever will be again. The birth of Jesus Christ is the single most important event in the history of the world. It is the crucial point of humanity . . . for all history up until that time moves toward it . . . and all history since that time moves away from it, making His arrival the very crossroads of time . . . and the world acknowledges this . . . for it sets it's calendar by His birth. Christ's coming down from His glory changed everything. All the kings of the earth, all the great and powerful leaders put together . . . have not affected the world like this child named Jesus . . . and mankind knows that He came. In fact, they're busy right now celebrating it. They know the name of the One who was born on Christmas day. . . and they know where He was born . . . They even know the approximate time, when it all took place. Most of them can even tell you about the various characters in the Christmas story. Although millions of people know who, when, where and what took place, the vast majority of them still miss the meaning of Christmas. The real story of Christmas is . . . why He came. Why Bethlehem? Why a manger? Why Shepherds? Why Wise Men? Why would God become a man?

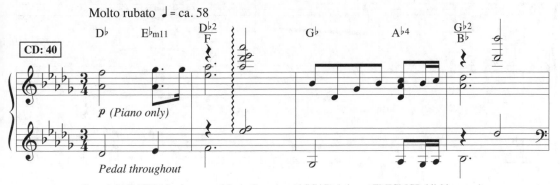

SOLO (freely)

Why would a King leave His throne and His

crown____ to come to earth as a

stran - ger? Oh,____ and why_____ would He

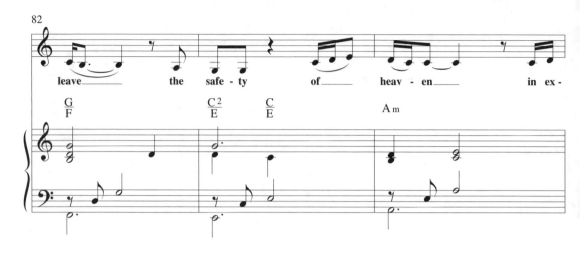

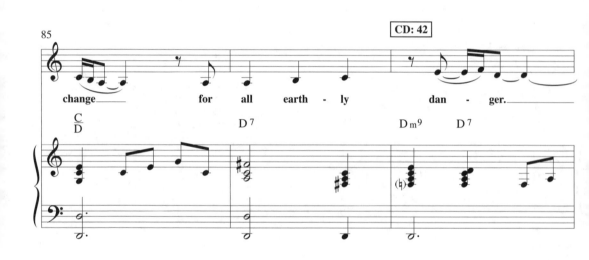

88
101

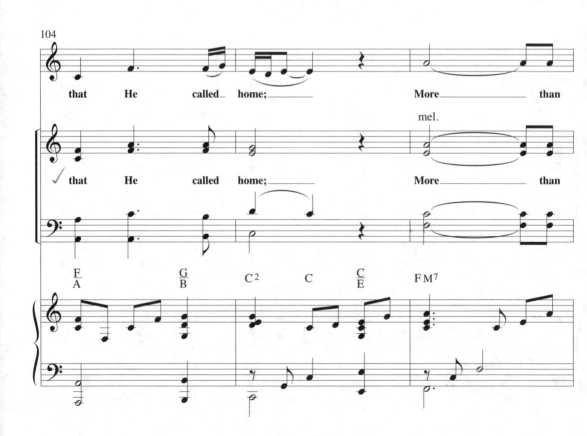

all of these He loved you and He loved me_____ and He

all of these He loved you and He loved me_____ and He

left it all be-cause He loved us more._____

left it all be-cause He loved us more._____

90

92

96

Glory

includes
Glory
Angels We Have Heard on High
Hark! the Herald Angels Sing
Amen

Arr. by Mike Speck

2nd Time

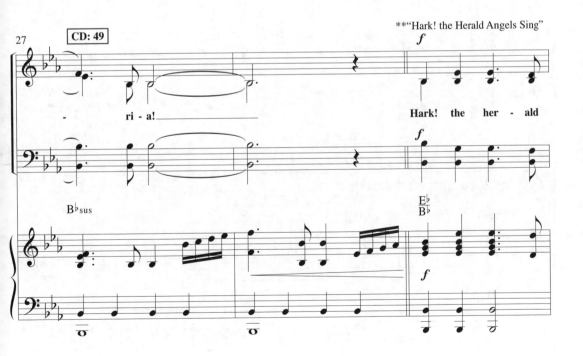

an - gels sing,

"Glo - ry to the new -

CD: 50

born King!"

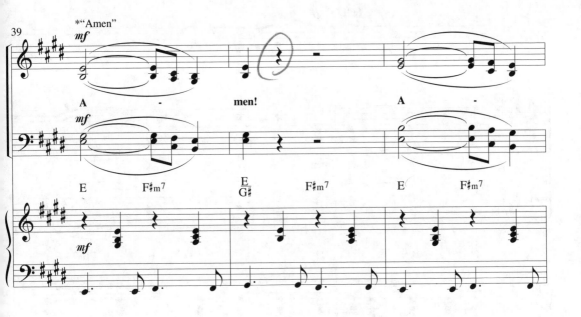

106

108

The Story That Never Grows Old Underscore
The Story That Never Grows Old

Words and Music by
CINDI BALLARD,
MATT GARINGER
and WAYNE HAUN
Arr. by Mike Speck

(Without music)

WORSHIP LEADER: Glory, glory, glory to the newborn King! The prophet said He would be called Emmanuel, which means God with us. God, who spoke everything into existence . . . the One who holds all there is in its place . . . left heaven and came to earth to become one of us. *(Music begins)* God . . . now as a man . . . tastes our frailties and our weaknesses, our struggles and disappointments . . . what it's like to feel alone . . . to cry from sorrow and grief . . . Yes, He lived as one of us . . . yet He had a far greater reason for leaving His throne. He came from the glories of Heaven because He so loved you and me and knew that He was the only One who could rescue us. He loved us so much that He willingly gave His life on a cross. That was His mission from the beginning. Had there not been a cross, there would never have been a manger . . . He was born in Bethlehem to be our sacrifice . . . our Savior. And for all who put their trust in this infant King, God is no longer a stranger, but a Father who is with us always. This is what Christmas is all about. It is the greatest story ever told . . . a story that no matter how many times we tell it, it never grows old. For those of us who have lost hope . . . for those longing for peace and relief...for those weary from the storms of life . . . for those who will face this Christmas with one less loved one around the tree . . . we can take comfort . . . we can find strength . . . we can rest and rejoice in knowing that Bethlehem shouts "we are so loved."

Molto rubato ♩ = ca. 86
*"I Love to Tell the Story"

[CD: 53]

Pedal throughout

CD: 54 *"The Story That Never Grows Old"

Heartfelt ♩ = ca. 74

"... storms of life ..."

"...we are so loved."

1. Year af-ter year as we cel-e-brate the sea-son,— some-

112

times   we lose the   joy   or for - get   the rea - son   why.

But   hold - ing___ the foun - da - tion___   of our earth - ly___   cel - e -

CD: 55

bra - tion___   is the   sto - ry of a King   who came___   to die.

114

sto - ry____ ev - er told._____ And the

sto - ry____ ev - er told._____ And the

an - gels still sing____ of the joy sal - va - tion

an - gels still sing____ of the joy sal - va - tion

2. When we____ look back on____ the mem-o-ries___ of

Christ-mas,__ so man-y____ of our loved ones___ have

made____ their jour-ney____ home.____ But

118

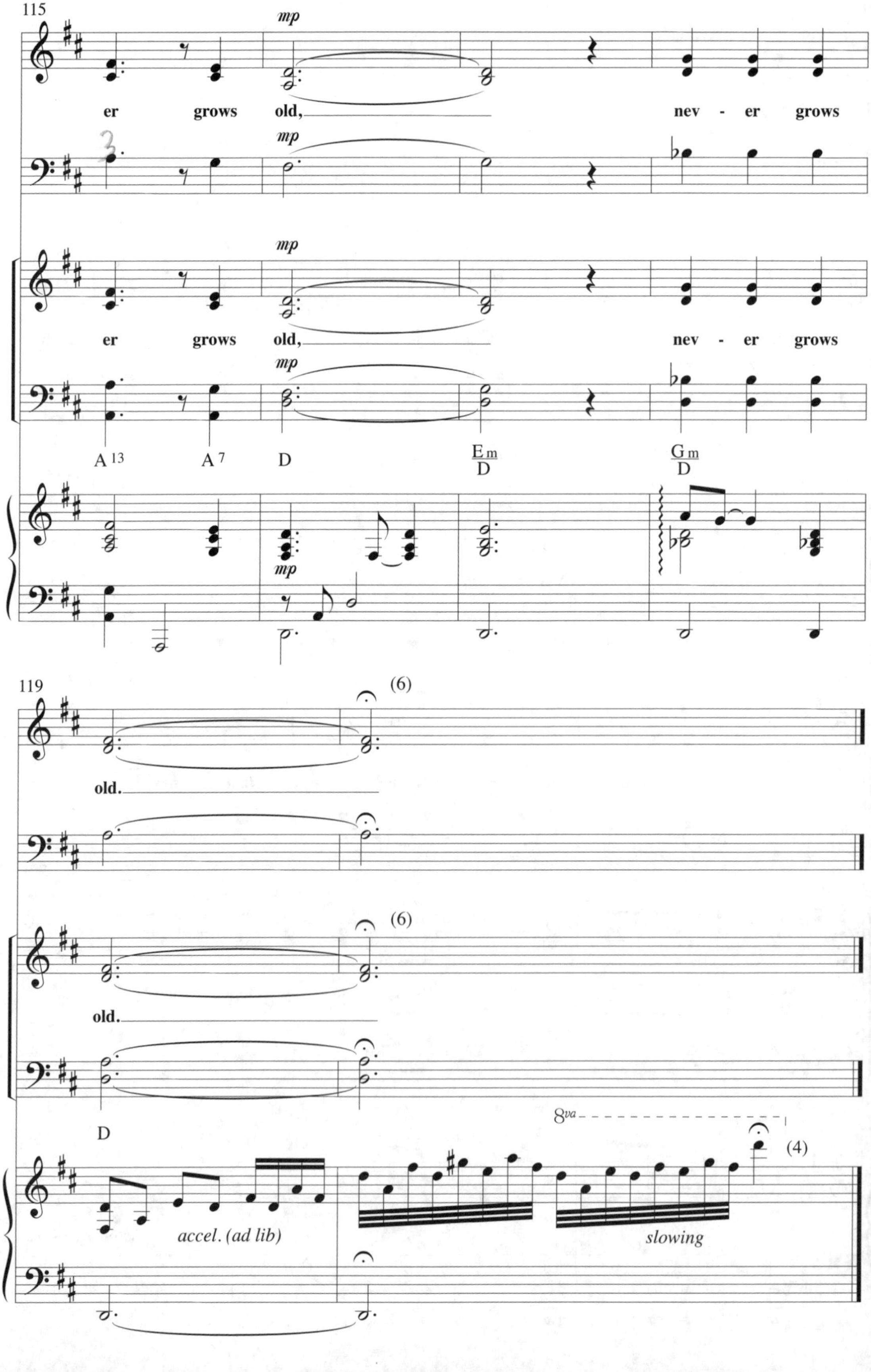
115
mp
er grows old, nev - er grows
mp
mp
er grows old, nev - er grows
mp
A13 A7 D Em/D Gm/D
mp
119
(6)
old.
(6)
old.
D
8va
(4)
accel. (ad lib)
slowing

Down from His Glory Finale

includes
Heaven Rejoices
Light of the Stable
Pat-a-Pan
For unto Us a Child Is Born
Glory
He Loved Us More
More than Wonderful
Down from His Glory

Arr. by Mike Speck

(Music begins)

WORSHIP LEADER: Let's rejoice with the angels of heaven. And let's thank the Lord for the gift of Christmas . . . our Redeemer . . . our Savior, who came down from His glory!

With energy! ♩ = ca. 107

*"Heaven Rejoices"

124

132

the Might-y God,   the   ev-er-last-ing Fa-ther,   the Prince of Peace,   the

ev-er-last-ing Fa-ther,   the Prince   of   Peace!

CD: 63

134

136

138

* **CD: 66**

*"Down from His Glory"

*Optional Reprise begins in measure 132.

*Words by WILLIAM E. BOOTH-CLIBBORN; Music by EDUARDO di CAPUA. Arr. © 2011 PsalmSinger Music/BMI
(admin. by Music Services). All rights reserved.

137

dore Him, my breath my sun - shine,

Fm   B♭   Fm

140

my all in all.   The great Cre - a - tor

B♭7   B♭6 B♭6/A♭ Gm7   Cm7   C♭

144   rit.

(a few sopranos)

be - came my Sav - ior   and all God's full - ness

F∅7   E♭/B♭   F°/C♭ Cm Fm7

rit.

FOR INFORMATION AND BOOKINGS CONTACT:

Mike Speck Ministries

P.O. Box 2609

Lebanon, TN 37088

(615) 449-1888